# HOW TO GET HONEST
# REVIEWS

"In this informative, easy-to-read book, Shelley Hitz and Heather Hart not only share a wealth of ideas as to how to get honest reviews, they also share why having book reviews is so important and how reviews can have a positive (or negative) effect on your book sales. Readers will LOVE the comprehensive list of places they can go online to get honest reviews for their books. I was excited to discover many online communities of authors who are dedicated to helping other authors. This book is based on practical advice from two educators who are dedicated to supporting authors on their success journey."

- D'vorah Lansky, M.Ed., and bestselling author of
Book Marketing Made Easy,
www.BookMarketingMadeEasy.com

"Shelley and Heather have done it again. This easy-to-follow guide gives you the resources you need to get your book dozens of reviews. I fully recommend 'How to Get Honest Reviews' for any author looking to separate from the pack."

- Bryan Cohen
www.BuildCreativeWritingIdeas.com

"This might sound like hyperbole, but after reading 'How to Get Honest Reviews,' I couldn't help but thinking it should be called 'The Ultimate Guide to Getting Honest Reviews.' The section on how to develop your own book review program was outstanding. I really liked the step by step approach the authors shared about how they started their own successful book review program, including samples of emails you can model, what resources to use and exactly how to set up your program. They didn't leave anything out. As they say, book reviews are like gold for authors and I believe any new or experienced author will benefit by studying Hart's and Hitz's system."

- Denise Wakeman, Online Business Strategist
www.DeniseWakeman.com

# HOW TO GET HONEST REVIEWS

## BOOK MARKETING SURVIVAL GUIDE V.1

Shelley Hitz and Heather Hart

Body and Soul Publishing
Colorado Springs, CO

Shelley Hitz
P.O. Box 6542
Colorado Springs, CO 80934
www.trainingauthors.com

Earnings Disclaimer: There is no promise or representation that you will make a certain amount of sales, or any sales, as a result of using the techniques that are outlined within this book. Any earnings, revenue, or results using these marketing strategies are strictly estimates and there is no guarantee that you will have the same results. You accept the risk that the earnings and income statements differ by individual. The use of our information, products and services should be based on your own due diligence and you agree that we are not liable for your success or failure.

Full Disclosure: Some of the links in this book may be affiliate links (excluding any and all links to Amazon) and we may earn a small commission when you make a purchase through them. By law (FTC), we must disclose this. However, we want to ensure you that we only endorse products and services we believe in and would or do use ourselves.

Book Layout ©2013 Book Design Templates
www.trainingauthors.com/booktemplates

Ordering Information:
Quantity sales. Special discounts are available on quantity purchases by corporations, associations, and others. For details, contact the "Special Sales Department" at the address above.

How to Get Honest Reviews / Shelley Hitz and Heather Hart. -- 1st ed.

ISBN-13: 978-0692022337
ISBN-10: 0692022333

# TABLE OF CONTENTS

# Before You Begin

If you are just getting started on your book marketing journey, we highly recommend reading the "Gear Up" post on our blog before you begin this book. That post will give you a good understanding of the foundation needed to successfully market your book.

Check out our four tips for beginners here:
www.trainingauthors.com/book-marketing-journey

# WAIT!

*Before you dig in to the information in this book,*
*how would you like to score a $27 author training course - FREE?*

*Do you need help coming up with a*
*book marketing plan that works for you?*

*We want to give you our master book marketing plan template with*
*a PDF training report free of charge.*

*Why?*

*Simply because we enjoy helping authors succeed.*

*Claim your free copy at the link below:*
*www.trainingauthors.com/newsletter*

# PART ONE

# Getting Started

# CHAPTER ONE

# Why Honest Reviews Are Important

Getting reviews for your book is an essential part of the publishing and marketing process. However, this is a step that many authors choose to skip or ignore. I believe this happens because of the reasons I have listed below.

1. Authors underestimate the importance and power of customer reviews.

   OR

2. Authors know the importance of reviews, but do not know where to start.

The good news?

*We address both of these issues within this book.*

## Why Are Reviews Important?

First of all, reviews help customers make buying decisions online. In fact, a research study[i] conducted by Dimensional Research showed that 90% of customers reported that reading positive reviews online impacted their buying decisions. In the same way, 86% of customers said that reading negative reviews online impacted their buying decisions as well.

Personally, I know that I (Shelley) am impacted by reading reviews online when making my purchasing decisions. Many times, I will skim the positive reviews and then go straight to the negative reviews to see what people do not like about the product I am researching.

As an author, I make it a goal to have a minimum of 5-10 reviews posted online for each of my published books prior to a book launch. After getting 10 reviews, I then allow the reviews to come in organically.

When I see an Amazon book sales page without any reviews, it reminds me of a ghost town.

*No one is there.*

Reviews provide social proof that people are actually buying and reading your book. If you have no reviews or very few reviews, it may cause your potential customers to wonder if your book is even worth reading.

Finally, there are certain advertising opportunities you will miss out on if you do not have a minimum of 10 reviews. For example, Ereader News Today (ENT) has a bargain book of the day promotion they offer to authors. When our books are featured on ENT, we usually sell hundreds of copies, which I consider a success. However, your book needs a minimum of 10 reviews in order to even be considered for this promotion. There are also other opportunities you will miss out on if you do not have a certain number of reviews.

Therefore, make sure to do your part to get honest book reviews. It does take effort on your part, but it is well worth it!

## Why Does Honesty Matter?

There are a ton of different options available to get reviews for your book. In this book, we will only cover options that provide honest reviews. We never recommend paying for a review or asking someone to write a review without first reading your book. There are two main reasons for that.

1. Dishonest reviews can ruin your credibility, making readers doubt you as an author as well as the quality of your book.

2. Dishonest reviews can cause repercussions from Amazon and other retailers—including the deletion of your books and Amazon account.

You should also consider that dishonest reviews are unethical and illegal. The Federal Trade Commission has specific rules for review products that you must adhere to as an author (more on this later). Dishonest reviews that violate their guidelines can bring legal ramifications and cost you thousands of dollars.

*Join us in this book as we take you step-by-step through the process of how to get honest reviews.*

# CHAPTER TWO

# Know that You Will Get a Variety of Reviews

When writing, publishing, and marketing your book it is good to know upfront that you will get both positive and negative reviews. After pouring your time and talent into your book (and some of your hard earned money), it is natural to want to see all 4 and 5 star reviews. However, the reality is that you will NOT please every reader who buys your book. Even the very best authors still get 1, 2, and 3 star reviews on their books.

I (Shelley) remember vividly one of the first bad reviews I received. I was devastated for days. However, I now understand and expect some low reviews on my books. I do not let it get me down like I did at first.

## Helpful Reviews on Amazon

Did you know that Amazon customers can vote a review as helpful or not? At the bottom of each review is this question:

*- Was this review helpful? Yes or No*

You can click on the "Yes" or "No" buttons to let Amazon know which reviews are most helpful. They will then list the reviews that get the most "Yes" votes first on your book sales page.

## Why Negative Reviews May Be Beneficial

Sometimes negative reviews can actually be helpful. If your book has all 5 star reviews, people may think your reviews are only from supporters: your family and friends.

Therefore, I encourage you to not be afraid of getting negative reviews. Expect that they will come and then move on. If you have written a good book, good reviews will continue to come in faster than the bad reviews and your overall rating will still remain high.

## Should You Respond to Reviews?

If you ask 100 authors this question, you will be given many different responses.

## - *No*

Some authors argue that you should never respond to a review. Instead of responding yourself, they would encourage you to let your fans defend you. Sometimes you can appear desperate for approval when you reply to bad reviews to try to convince the reader to change their opinion.

I do have one piece of advice for you.

Do not try to argue with someone who posted a negative review on your book. It can easily become a heated back-and-forth argument, which can make you look bad. Plus, it is very hard to reason with someone who is responding out of emotion. They are not reasoning with their mind and intellect, but their emotions. Therefore, you will most likely not be able to change their mind anyway.

Instead of trying to defend yourself, simply accept the negative review and let it go. Do not allow negative reviews to define who you are as an author.

## -*Yes*

Some authors argue there are times it is acceptable to respond to a review. I have observed certain authors who will respond by thanking the reader for their review. It can be done in a professional way and simply lets the reader know that you appreciate them taking the time to post their review of your book. Also, when you respond to a review it lets your readers know that you are a real person.

Some authors will respond to reviews in order to address a valid concern the reader has with their book. They respond and thank them for their response and feedback. The author may even take action based upon the review and then reply to let the reviewer know the changes that were made.

However, more often than not, it is usually best to not respond to your book reviewers.

Now that we have covered some of the basics of what to expect with reviews, Heather is going to discuss where readers can post reviews online.

# CHAPTER THREE

# Places for Readers to Post Reviews

Shelley has already covered why reviews are important, but there are countless places where book reviews can be posted online. In this chapter, I (Heather) am going to cover some of the places where readers can post reviews, as well as the benefits of having reviews scattered across the web.

Where you want book reviews posted will depend a lot on your niche, audience, and marketing strategy. Where does your target audience go for book reviews? This is something you will want to know before approaching reviewers. Amazon reviews are big, but readers also hangout on sites like Goodreads, Barnes & Noble, and other niche related sites.

By knowing your target audience, you can figure out where it will be most helpful to have reviews posted for your book. Then, when you request reviews, you can include links to one or two of the most important places for your target audience. Once you hit your target number of reviews, you can switch out your links in review requests and start building reviews on another website or start letting reviews come in organically.

Below, I will cover several places where readers can post reviews for books of all genres. I will start with some of the most well-known places and then cover a few less-known, but still worthy of looking into, options.

## Amazon

Most authors report that the majority of their online sales come from Amazon, and, when it comes to discussing books online, most other websites that promote books will link back to it as well. Therefore, we believe that Amazon should be the main focus when soliciting book reviews.

As Shelley mentioned earlier, several websites that do book promotion even have stipulations regarding Amazon reviews; e.g., they will only list your book if it has over x number of reviews on Amazon and an average of at least 4 stars. But there's also the readers to consider. If Amazon is selling the most books online for most authors, it stands a good chance that their reviews are the most read. Having a high number of reviews and a good star-rating on Amazon gives your book credibility.

Readers can also filter search results on Amazon by their average customer review rating. Without any reviews, your book will automatically be left out of those results. Having at least one four or five star review will get you included in all the search results for your book's keywords.

Obviously, Amazon is not the only place where readers can post reviews, but it is certainly one place you will want to consider when deciding where you would like readers to post their reviews.

**Amazon Review Guidelines**

Amazon does have strict rules for soliciting reviews that you need to know as an author. Here are just a few:

1. You are not allowed to give anything in exchange for a review other than a free copy of your book. You cannot send gift cards, pay someone to review your book, or even do a review exchange with another author according to their terms.

2. In order to post a review on Amazon, the reader has to have purchased something from Amazon in the past. If you open a brand new Amazon account, you cannot post a review until you make a purchase where money is exchanged. Downloading free books doesn't count. Claiming a book that someone else gifted you doesn't count either. You have to make an actual purchase before you can post a review.

3. You cannot review your own book on Amazon, or the book of a family member. In other words, you should not ask your mom to review your book on Amazon.

4. According to Amazon's terms of service, they own the copyright to reviews posted on their site. Therefore, if reviewers publish a review on Amazon as well as their blog or another retailer, it should not be the exact same content in both places.

5. You cannot review books that you have a financial interest in or books that directly compete with yours within your niche. Some authors are now reporting[ii] that their reviews are being removed from books of their peers.

Shelley e-mailed Amazon for further clarification on what "directly competing" means as authors do read and review books. We wanted to make sure to give you correct information and be within their terms of service. This was their reply:

====================

"We appreciate your desire to follow our guidelines when leaving reviews on other books. As previously mentioned, our guidelines prohibit authors or other people with financial interest in a book from posting any reviews for their own books or negative reviews for directly competing books. This restriction does not prohibit you from reviewing books within your same genre or category, however. We are more concerned with books which compete for the same niche within a genre. Anything thematically similar or otherwise seen as though it might be competition in sales is considered off-limits to reviews from you.

Our Customer Review feature was created to allow our customers to offer honest and unbiased opinions to other customers. We feel that allowing authors, artists and publishers to review their own or competing titles would be contrary to the goal of offering independent customer feedback. Your participation in leaving reviews is important to us, and we really do appreciate that you've reached out to us to make sure that you are within these guidelines.

I hope this helps further explain and clarify our guidelines on leaving reviews on directly competing products. We won't be able to provide further insight or explanation of this policy. Please, feel free to refer to our review guidelines, which can be found here:
www.amazon.com/review-guidelines

=====================

Even though "directly competing" authors are unable to post reviews for you, you can ask them for endorsements. You can then put these endorsements in the beginning of your book, on the book cover, in the "Editorial Reviews" section on your book's sales page on Amazon and/or on your website. You can see how Shelley did that with her book, *Marketing Your Book on Amazon*, at:
www.amazon.com/dp/B009SGXWM0

You can read all of Amazon's review guidelines at:
www.amazon.com/gp/community-help/customer-reviews-guidelines

## Barnes & Noble

Barnes & Noble is one of the few major book store chains left. If you have your book listed in their online database, building reviews on their website can be helpful—especially if you promote your book on their site regularly.

If NOOK sales are a priority to you, then getting reviews on Barnes & Noble is a must. If your book is enrolled in KDP Select, but the paperback version is available on Barnes & Noble, it may not be a high of a priority for you. However, you may still want to consider it.

The secret behind Barnes & Noble reviews is that the star rating is more important than the numbers. If you are near a computer, search for "teen girl devotional books." This should pull up three of the books in our internationally best-selling series, *Teen Devotionals... for Girls!*

You will notice that two of our three books have 5 star reviews. It will not tell you how many reviews they have, only that they are rated at 5 stars. So when a customer is searching for a good book on Barnes & Noble, this is something they will see.

### Barnes & Noble Review Guidelines

Barnes & Noble does not require reviewers to include text with their reviews. Therefore, readers can leave a star rating (as long as they are signed into their account) without typing out an actual review. The rules section of their website does say an actual review is required, however we have seen several reviews come through with only stars and a message saying no text was provided.

Readers must sign up for a free Barnes & Noble online account to post a review, but they are not required to make an actual purchase or provide any financial information.

You can find all of the Barnes & Noble review rules at: www.barnesandnoble.com/reviews/review_rules.asp

## Other Online Retailers

Besides Amazon and Barnes & Noble, there are other online retailers where you can accumulate reviews. We recommend building reviews on any of the platforms on which you promote your book regularly.

Most online retailers require readers to have an account before posting a review, but not all sites allow reviews to be posted directly. Some of the retailers that do allow reviews include: Smashwords, the iBooks Store, and Audible.

## Goodreads

Goodreads and Amazon are the two sites we focus on the most when we solicit reviews. If you are not already familiar with Goodreads, it is a social networking site that revolves around books—and has over 15 million members. Besides having different groups and forums readers can join, it also allows them to let their friends know what they are reading, follow other readers reviews, and so much more.

There are several great things about Goodreads reviews. The first is that readers can mark your book as currently-reading and have it displayed on their profile. Next, readers can follow reviews written by other readers—so when someone reviews your book, anyone following their reviews will get a notification. It will also show up in their profile feed with a list of books they have read, as well as give them the option to post about it on Facebook and recommend it to their friends.

Another benefit to reviews on Goodreads is that they will feed their reviews to other places online via the ISBN. At one point in time, the only reviews that appeared on Kobo were Goodreads reviews. They discontinued this in 2013, but have said they will be re-adding the Goodreads reviews and launching their own review program in the near future. The MyBookTable plugin also imports Goodreads reviews to your book page. Shelley has used this plugin on her author hub website and you can see an example of a book page at: shelleyhitz.com/books/book-marketing-success-bundle

### Goodreads Review Guidelines

Goodreads reviews can be a star rating, a sentence, or 10 pages long. They value honest opinions and do not have the limitations on their reviews that Amazon does.

You can find a copy of the Goodreads review guidelines at: www.Goodreads.com/review/guidelines

## LibraryThing and Shelfari

LibraryThing and Shelfari are both similar platforms to Goodreads. LibraryThing reports just over 1.5 million users and Shelfari boasts 500,000 monthly visitors. While not as large as Goodreads, those are still large audiences of readers, and while Shelfari is owned by Amazon, they do not link their reviews.

## The Book Club Network

The Book Club Network (also known as BookFun) focuses on Christian books and is owned by the Book Fun Magazine. They do a ton of book giveaways, let readers vote for the book of the month, and other fun stuff.

BookFun is not a retailer, so reviews on this site work a little differently. Instead of leaving a review on a book, you leave it in a group. They have one main group for reviews (www.bookfun.org/group/reviews-by-readers-only-group-public?commentId=5748904%3AComment%3A244869), but they also have groups listed by publisher, genre, book clubs, etc. If you wanted a reader to post a review to this site, it's best to pick the group you want it posted in in advance.

One thing to note is that they do not allow authors to post links to books on Amazon or other retailers as they have their own retail store, Deeper Shopping. If you do post other links, you may get your account closed.

## Blogs and Websites

Last, but not least, are blogs and websites. Most traditional publishers have or use professional review programs just for bloggers. They usually ask bloggers to post reviews on one major retailer and their own blog. The reason behind this is that bloggers build up a following of people who know, like, and trust them—just like we do as authors.

Having reviews on a blog or website, not only gets your book in front of their following, but it gets the honest opinion of a trusted source right there with it. Asking a reviewer to post a review on their own blog or website is 100% okay, and can be a great idea. Just note that Amazon's terms of service say they own the reviews posted on their site. If readers post reviews in both places, the review should be somewhat different on their blog than what they post on Amazon.

## It All Comes Down To This

Having book reviews scattered across the web increases the credibility of your book. If your book only has reviews on Amazon, readers on Goodreads may never find it, and those who shop on Barnes & Noble may pass it by.

It comes back to what Shelley wrote in the beginning of this book about the benefits of having reviews. The more reviews you have, the more places you have them in, the better off you will be. There is no such thing as having too many reviews.

# PART TWO

# How to Get Honest Reviews

CHAPTER FOUR

# Sphere of Influence

One of the questions we often get about reviews is simply, "How do I get more book reviews?" Therefore, in this section, we will show you 7 different ways to solicit reviews that we have used successfully in the past.

The first way to get reviews is to simply ask people within your sphere of influence—the people you have contact with or influence over on a regular basis.

## The People You Know

You can start by asking people you know personally if they would be interested in reviewing your book. These can be co-workers, friends, church members, etc. Just make sure they know you are seeking honest reviews and never ask someone to review your book without reading it first.

## Your Online Following

Other options for soliciting reviews might include asking your online following. If you have a following on any of the social media sites you use, you can post a status update letting them know you are seeking reviews. (Note: We will talk more about soliciting social media in an upcoming chapter.)

If you have an e-mail list of readers, you can send out an e-mail asking for reviews. You might offer free review copies to the first 5 people that respond, or even ask those who have already read your book if they would be willing to take a minute to review it online for you. You can do the same thing on your blog if you have one.

## Your Readers

Another option is to encourage readers to leave reviews by adding a simple request in the back of your book. Here is an example from the back of K.M. Weiland's books (fiction and non-fiction):

> **Note From the Author**: Reviews are gold to authors! If you've enjoyed this book, would you consider rating it and reviewing it on www.Amazon.com?

You can also replace the link to Amazon with the direct link to your eBook's listing. (*Note:* You cannot use an Amazon affiliate link within your eBook so the link needs to be a direct link to your book without your affiliate tag if you are an Amazon affiliate.)

*Tip:* For more information on what to include in the back of your book, I recommend this article Shelley wrote: thefutureofink.com/back-of-your-ebook

If the reader is reading a Kindle eBook on a Kindle device, they will automatically be prompted to leave a review when they finish the book. However, many people don't flip all the way through the back matter to the very end and may miss that feature. Having a prompt directly after the main story or content can increase the number of reviews you get.

Adding a note can also increase the reviews you get from non-Kindle readers. If your book is available in paperback or on another platform, having a request can give people who would not normally think to write a review the inspiration they need—especially if they enjoyed your book.

Just note that if your book is available through Smashwords, you cannot link directly to Amazon as that violates Smashwords' terms of service. You can link to your book's sales page on your website, include a link to Goodreads, or just mention that they can post reviews on Amazon.com without including a link. For their convenience, and a higher review rate, I do highly recommend including the link. If it is already there, it takes less work for them and they will be more likely to click through and write a short review.

## Recap

Just to recap, to get reviews from readers within your sphere of influence you can:

- Ask people you know personally
- Post requests on social media
- Send an e-mail
- Publish a request on your blog and/or
- Add a note to the back of your book

There is one more way to get reviews from readers in your sphere of influence, but we will share more about this when we discuss developing a book review program at the end of this section. We are saving the best for last!

# CHAPTER FIVE

# Amazon Reviewers

There are many options for getting book reviews. In this chapter, I (Shelley) am going to focus on how to find and contact Amazon book reviewers. I have done this manually in the past and have had some success. Not every reviewer will e-mail you back or post a review about your book, but this is an option you can try. However, whatever you do, please do not spam these reviewers or add them to an e-mail list without their permission.

## #1: Search Amazon Top Reviewers

Go to: www.amazon.com/review/top-reviewers

You can then search the top reviewers on Amazon. You will then need to check their profile and see if they review books similar to yours. This process takes time and is tedious but can yield results for you.

## #2: Check Similar Books to Find Amazon Book Reviewers

Another option is to find a popular book with a lot of reviews that is similar to yours. Then manually check the profiles for that left reviews for this book to see if they have an e-mail address or a website link listed in their public profile on Amazon. To find their public profile, simply click on their name listed with the review.

If they do have a website URL, you can often find a contact form on their site in order to get in touch with them.

This process is also time consuming and something you might consider outsourcing to a VA (virtual assistant) or someone on Fiverr.com.

## #3: Use the Review Grabber Tool from Author Marketing Club

I had a free membership with Author Marketing Club (AMC) for over a year and recently decided to try their premium membership. My favorite tool in their premium membership is the Review Grabber Tool. You enter a keyword and then it brings up books on Amazon. You can then click a few buttons and it will bring back the reviewers that have either an e-mail address or a website in their profile.

*I love this tool!*

It is such a time saver and allows me to contact Amazon reviewers without investing much of my time—time I could spend on writing more books! They even give you a copy and paste sample e-mail template that you can then use and customize with your information when contacting reviewers.

You can see this tool in action on YouTube, as well as a tour of all of the premium membership benefits, at:

www.trainingauthors.com/amcvideo

# CHAPTER SIX

# Social Media

Social media is a great place to solicit book reviews—even if you do not have a following. There are a number of options when it comes to gathering reviews on social platforms. We already mentioned asking your following for reviews earlier in this section, but you can also post reviews in different social media groups and forums.

Just make sure to read the rules for each group before posting your review request and do not spam. Otherwise, you may have your post deleted and/or get banned from the group. For more tips on what NOT to post on social media, read Shelley's article at: thefutureofink.com/marketing-your-book

## Facebook

Facebook groups are a great way to get reviews. There are a several groups dedicated to book reviews that have a high number of readers. We have listed some of them for you below:

**Review Seekers:**

www.facebook.com/groups/reviewseekers

**I need Book Reviews:**

A review exchange community.
www.facebook.com/groups/writersneedreviews

**Short eBook Reviews:**

This group does reviews of short eBooks on Amazon.
www.facebook.com/groups/267671490031920

**Reviewers Roundup:**

This is a group to both post and solicit book reviews.
www.facebook.com/groups/ReviewersRoundup

**Writers, Readers, Researchers, and Reviewers:**

This group is for anyone with an interest in writing, reading, researching and reviewing books, stories, articles, films, historical periods and events and other literature.
www.facebook.com/groups/441618909278671

**Independent Authors eBooks and reviews please!**

This is a family friendly group for indie authors to share and promote their books and blogs with an emphasis on helping each other get reviews.
www.facebook.com/groups/mynewbook2

**Non Fiction Book Reviews:**

A review exchange group specifically for non-fiction, how-to, and children's book authors.
www.facebook.com/groups/467373490035139

**Christian Book Reviews:**

A review group specifically for Christian books.
www.facebook.com/groups/108300165857067

**Christian Review of Books:**

Another group specifically for reviews of Christian books.
www.facebook.com/groups/121238177904758

With the right search terms, you can find even more review groups on Facebook. Some are niche specific, others are not, and they all have their own list of rules. As we mentioned previously, make sure you read through the requirements for each group before posting.

## LinkedIn

If you are a member of LinkedIn, they also have a number of book review groups (if you are not a member, they offer a free membership). I have listed a couple of them for you below, just remember, as with the Facebook groups, read the group rules before posting.

**Book Reviewers:**

A group where book reviewers meet up and share information. I've seen both review requests and review exchanges posted here. www.linkedin.com/groups/Book-Reviewers-1521067

**Authors Book Reviews:**

A group for authors and readers. You can share book reviews, request reviews, but no books with adult content are allowed. www.linkedin.com/groups/Authors-Book-Reviews

You can also search for groups in your niche to target readers who are more your target market. I (Heather) have often gotten the best reviews on LinkedIn by offering a free review copy in a discussion thread when a reader was asking for book recommendations or had a question that I covered in-depth in my book.

*Warning:* You should avoid answering a question in a forum with, "I answered this question in my book: link to purchase." It is not helpful and does not help readers to view you in a good light. Offering free review copies is acceptable, but even then I usually answer the question first and then offer a free review copy.

## Google+

Google+ also has review communities that you can join. I have listed three below, but you can also search for others that might be more niche specific. Again, be sure to read the group description and follow any rules that are set forward.

**Reader, Writer, Reviewer Co-op:**

A community for readers and writers exchanging their writings and helping each other with online reviews.

plus.google.com/u/0/communities /100528034080476038209

**Book Reviewers:**

This is a place to introduce your books, share your reviews, post give-aways, author interviews, or just simply be creative.

plus.google.com/u/0/communities/ 100709131316639681588

**Kindle & eBook Writers and Reviewers:**

You can post review requests here, but no more than one post per day.

plus.google.com/u/0/communities/ 115033069731883932764

## Goodreads

Goodreads is a platform developed specifically around readers, so it is always a good go-to place for any type of marketing. I covered the benefits of collecting book reviews on Goodreads in part one, but it is also good to note that, from my experience, reviewers on Goodreads will post their reviews both on Goodreads and on a retailer website or their own blog.

Goodreads has thousands of groups full of readers, and many are dedicated to book reviews. I have listed close to a dozen for you here, but Goodreads is growing and new groups are created each day. And, as I said, there are already thousands of groups available, so I could never list them all.

**Review Group:**

A group for self-published and indie authors to post review requests.
www.Goodreads.com/group/show/78683-review-group

**Genre Specific Review Groups:**

This is another group for indie authors to request reviews.
www.Goodreads.com/group/show/100482-genre-specific-review-groups

**Goodreads Reviewers' Group:**

This group helps to bring Reviewers and Authors together. Authors can make their own thread in the Author's folder to find reviewers for their book.
www.Goodreads.com/group/show/105786-Goodreads-reviewers-group

**Authors Helping Authors:**

This group is a place where authors and bloggers can come together and help one another out. Review requests are welcomed and encouraged.
www.Goodreads.com/group/show/94882-authors-helping-authors

**Helping hand to new authors:**

This is an open group where authors can promote free books, giveaways, and request reviews. As well as swap book marketing tips.
www.Goodreads.com/group/show/58236-helping-hand-to-new-authors

**Advanced Copies for Review & Book Giveaways:**

You can post new releases, giveaways, and book reviews and review requests here.

www.Goodreads.com/group/show/58575-advanced-copies-for-review-book-giveaways

**Authors & Reviewers:**

Pretty self explanatory.

www.Goodreads.com/group/show/103713-authors-reviewers

**Fantasy Authors Review & Blog Community:**

A review exchange community for fantasy authors.

www.Goodreads.com/group/show/125588-fantasy-authors-review-blog-community

**Addicted to Book Reviews:**

Another book review group on Goodreads.

www.Goodreads.com/group/show/84740-addicted-to-book-reviews

**ARC of Authors:**

This community is only for advance review copies (ARC) of fiction books. Books must be listed and review copies sent out before the books official launch.

www.Goodreads.com/group/show/93438-arc-of-authors

**Author/Blogger Network:**

This group is for authors and bloggers in the young adult and middle grade genre. Review requests are welcomed and encouraged.

www.Goodreads.com/group/show/58989-author-blogger-network

These lists could go on and on and on, but you now have plenty of resources to get you started in the right direction. In the next chapter, Shelley will cover how you can submit your book to a review site, Readers' Favorite.

# CHAPTER SEVEN

# Readers' Favorite

Readers' Favorite is a book review and award site. We have used their free service several times for our books. However, you can upgrade for a small fee to have your review prioritized and completed within two weeks. If you do upgrade, you are not paying for the review itself, but for the speed of the turnaround time. Yet, because Readers' Favorite offers this upgrade, they are unable to post their reviews on Amazon, but they do post their reviews on their website as well as six other places as follows:

1. Barnes & Noble
2. Google Books
3. Facebook
4. Twitter
5. Google Plus
6. Pinterest

They will only publicly post book reviews that receive a four or five star rating. Otherwise, they contact the author directly with constructive feedback on how they think your book could be improved. I appreciate this fact about Readers' Favorite as their goal is to share *honest* reviews for *quality* books to their readers.

If you do submit your book to Readers' Favorite and get a five star rating from them, you will receive a "Five Star" digital seal for your website and a high resolution seal that you can add to your print book cover.

Finally, I encourage you to submit your book to the Readers' Favorite annual book awards contest. Winning a book award can give you credibility as an author and allows you to add "award-winning author" to your bio.

Submit your book to Readers' Favorite for a review here: www.trainingauthors.com/readersfavorite

# CHAPTER EIGHT

# Blogs

Another option for soliciting reviews is to contact book bloggers. Book bloggers are readers who have their own blog or website where they post book reviews. Most book bloggers will post reviews on their blog as well as one or two other outlets, such as Amazon or Goodreads.

The main differences between having your book reviewed on a blog versus having it reviewed on a retail site, is that book bloggers tend to go into more detail and they usually have a following of readers who value their opinion.

Blog reviews are a great way to get your book in front of your target audience. If someone reads and enjoys your book and recommends it to their following on their blog, usually the people following them will like the same sort of books they do. So instead of randomly searching the category on Amazon, they have someone they know, like, and trust, recommending them a book in the genre they like to read.

We will go into contacting reviewers in great detail in the next section, but when approaching a blogger about reviewing your book you need to do so in a very personal, yet professional manner. Make sure to check and see if they read your genre before contacting them. Also, if your book is on a controversial or sensitive subject, you need to be sure the blogger you are contacting is an appropriate choice for your book.

While blog reviews can do amazing things for sales, they also have the power to do more harm than good if you go about it the wrong way. Bloggers have the right to say no to or ignore you. Do not contact them repeatedly and never write anything to them in an e-mail that you would not want published on their blog.

## Places to Find Blogs that Post Book Reviews

There are several different ways to find blogs in your niche that post book reviews. I (Heather) believe the very best way is to simply start following a few blogs in your niche and start interacting with the readers there. Once the author of the blog recognizes you, they may be more open to reviewing your book because they have a connection with you. You will also be able to communicate with other readers who follow their blog and network with them to find out about other blogs in your niche that may be willing to post a review for you.

I know that most authors only have so much time to dedicate to blog following, so if you are looking for some blogs to contact right away you will want to consider blog directories. There are two main blog directories that I find helpful when looking for book reviews.

### The Indie View

This website has a list of readers willing to review books by indie authors. It is updated regularly and very organized. It lets you know up front what genres the blog accepts, where they will post their reviews, and shares helpful links.

www.theindieview.com/indie-reviewers

### Book Reviewer Yellow Pages

This use to be Step-by-Step Self-Publishing, and has review sites listed alphabetical order.

http://www.bookrevieweryellowpages.com/reviewer-list.html

You can also look for blog directories in your niche to see if any of those bloggers offer book reviews, but the two above list sites that specifically do book reviews for authors.

## Another Option

Looking for bloggers to contact about getting your book reviewed can be a lot of work. For the launch of Shelley's book, *Marketing Your Book on Amazon,* she gave away an extra bonus to anyone who posted a review on their blog within a specific time frame after the launch. They then sent us the link to their review and we sent them a special bonus.

It worked out great, however we do mention it with caution as it is against Amazon's terms of service to provide anything in exchange for a book review other than a free copy of the book. So if you decide to try something like this, be sure to note that the entry is only applicable to reviews posted on private blogs. Most of Shelley's readers ended up posting both a review on their blog and an Amazon review, but because of Amazon's terms of service, it is important to note that the bonuses are only for the reviews posted on blogs.

If you do not have a special bonus you would like to give away, you may also consider doing a special giveaway and having readers enter by posting reviews of your book on their blog. You can have them leave the link to their post in the comments section of your own blog or e-mail it to you and then use a random number generator like Random.org to select the winner. Or you could use giveaway management tool such as RaffleCopter to collect the links and chose a winner.

Shelley is going to cover more ways that you can use giveaways to get reviews in the next chapter. So now that we have covered blog post reviews, I will turn it over to her.

# CHAPTER NINE

# Conduct Giveaways

Another way to get honest reviews is to conduct giveaways for your book. Conducting a giveaway does not guarantee you will get reviews, but often does yield results.

In this chapter, I (Shelley) am going to discuss four different types of giveaways you can conduct to get more reviews.

## #1: KDP Select

One way to get reviews for a book is to use Amazon's KDP Select program. This program launched in December of 2011 and I enrolled one of our books in the program in early January, 2012. In order to enroll your book in KDP Select, you have to agree to give KDP exclusive rights to your eBook. However, you can still publish print and AudioBook versions of your book when it is enrolled in KDP Select.

Once your book is enrolled in KDP Select, you can choose to promote your book for free in the Kindle store for up to 5 days during your 90 day contract. The readers that download your book for free may post a review online after they finish reading it. Make sure to add a blurb at the end of your book that encourages them to post a review. We covered this in detail in the Sphere of Influence chapter under the heading "Your Readers."

**Note of caution**: When you run a free promotion, you may attract readers that are not your target audience. Therefore, this may result in receiving bad reviews if the book was not what they expected. However, I have personally found that the benefits of running a free promotion still outweigh the disadvantages.

You can get my 11-step checklist and 76+ places to promote your free KDP Select promotion at:
www.trainingauthors.com/47-places-to-submit-your-free-kdp-promotion-for-your-kindle-ebook

## #2: Goodreads Giveaways

Goodreads currently allows you to conduct print book giveaways on their site. I suggest you consider this option to get more exposure for your book and to potentially get more reviews.

Here are some important things to know about Goodreads giveaways:

- You must have published a print book in order to qualify. Do you still need to publish a print version of your book? If so, see our recommendations on how to self-publish your print book at: www.trainingauthors.com/printbooks

- To post a giveaway, login to Goodreads, and visit this link: www.Goodreads.com/giveaway/new
- To see a list of current giveaways, go here: www.Goodreads.com/giveaway
- Read this case study to find out how to get the best results with a Goodreads giveaway: www.novelpublicity.com/2012/02/how-to-run-a-Goodreads-giveaway-with-maximal-results-11-tips-we-know-youll-need

When running a Goodreads giveaway, I will often place a call to action in my book description for those who visit my giveaway to join my e-mail list. This helps me build a list of targeted readers that I can continue to build a relationship with where they grow to know, like, and trust me.

And do not forget to ask the winner to consider posting their honest review online once they finish reading your book.

When I conduct a Goodreads giveaway, I usually get hundreds of readers who enter my giveaway and mark the book as "to-read." This gives my book more exposure on the Goodreads platform as their activity is often posted on their personal profile.

You can see the giveaways I have conducted at: www.Goodreads.com/giveaway/created_by/6895795-shelley-hitz

*Other helpful links:*

- If you have not yet joined the Goodreads author program, you can find out how to apply here: www.Goodreads.com/author/program
- Find an exhaustive how-to document about Goodreads for authors here:
  www.Goodreads.com/author/how_to
- It is also recommend that every author review the Author Guidelines, as they detail what to do and what not to do on Goodreads:
  www.Goodreads.com/author/guidelines

## #3: How to Conduct a LibraryThing Giveaway

Have you heard of LibraryThing? Heather briefly mentioned it earlier, but LibraryThing is a website similar to Goodreads where readers can review books, interact with authors, and more. It is free to sign up as a member.

One of the benefits of LibraryThing is the ability to conduct eBook giveaways. Unlike Goodreads, where you have to give away print copies of your book, LibraryThing allows you to give away eBook, audiobook, or print copies.

I like this feature as it allows authors to conduct giveaways with no out of pocket expense. For example, you can give away Smashwords 100% off coupons or create eBook files to give away (i.e., PDF, .epub and/or .mobi files). These file types are covered in depth in a later chapter titled, "Types of Review Files to Send."

If you create your own files, you can either attach them to an e-mail or upload them to your hosting account and give the reader a download link. However, you can also conduct a print book or audiobook giveaway as well.

LibraryThing giveaways are an opportunity for authors to get more exposure and potentially more reviews. You can see the current list of giveaways on their site at:

www.librarything.com/er/giveaway/list.

**Please note:** If your book is enrolled in the KDP Select program, you will not be able to give the eBook version away on sites like Library-Thing. Therefore, one option is to initially publish your eBook on Kindle without enrolling it in the KDP Select program.

Then, conduct your giveaway on LibraryThing and solicit reviews. Once you have completed your giveaway, you can enroll your book in the KDP Select program at that time. This is what I did with the giveaway case study I share below.

### How to Conduct a LibraryThing Member Giveaway

To post a book for a Member Giveaway, at least one of the following must be true:

1. You are a LibraryThing Author.
2. You have at least 50 books in your LibraryThing account.
3. You have a paid LibraryThing account.

**Step #1: How to Become a LibraryThing Author**

The easiest way to conduct an eBook giveaway is to become a Library-Thing author. It is free and simple to do. First of all, you will need to sign up for a free member account.

Once you are signed in to your account, you will then need to search on LibraryThing.com for your author page by searching for your name. You can use the search box in the upper right hand corner of their website. If you already have an author page, you will see an "Is this you?" box in the upper right hand corner. You then click on that link to request author status. If you do not find your author page after searching on their site, you may need to add your book to their database first.

*More Resources:*

- Becoming a LibraryThing Author:
  www.librarything.com/blogs/librarything/2011/01/be-coming-a-librarything-author-just-got-easier
- LibraryThing Page for Authors:
  www.librarything.com/about/authors

**Step #2: How to Set Up Your LibraryThing Giveaway**

To set up your LibraryThing giveaway, go to this link and fill out their form: www.librarything.com/er_book.php?program=giveaway

When doing an eBook giveaway, I recommend giving away 100 copies. The giveaways are listed by the number of copies given and the date the giveaway ends. Therefore, the books with the most copies available will be listed closer to the top of the list and will therefore get more exposure.

You can also choose which countries you want to include for your giveaway. Personally, I chose all countries for my eBook giveaway to get the most exposure possible. Also make sure to check the box "requesting reviews" when filling out the form.

You can choose one week, two weeks, three weeks, or four weeks for your giveaway duration. I wanted to conduct my giveaway as quickly as possible so that I could then enroll my book in the KDP select program. Therefore, I chose the shortest duration possible: one week. But, it is up to you how long you want your giveaway to run.

In my giveaway description I made sure to let readers know these three things:

1. How the eBook would be delivered.
2. The type of book I was offering so I could attract my target audience.
3. That I was conducting the giveaway in order to get more reviews online.

Feel free to use my description below as an outline for your Library-Thing giveaways.

====================

The eBook will be delivered via a Smashwords coupon so you can choose the eBook format you prefer.

Please note: This is a Christian book.

We are giving away these books to increase the impact of the message of the book but also to get more reviews online. Reviews on Amazon, Goodreads and LibraryThing are appreciated.

====================

Once your giveaway has ended, you will then receive the names and e-mail addresses of those who requested your book. I typed up an e-mail and then copied and pasted it into each e-mail I sent to save time. If you use Gmail, you can also use canned responses to save time sending the e-mails.

**My Giveaway Results**

I conducted a LibraryThing eBook giveaway on 12/6/12 for my book, *Unshackled and Free: True Stories of Forgiveness* and offered up to 100 copies.

Here are my results:

- 34 readers requested the book.
- We received 3 new reviews on Amazon, 4 reviews on LibraryThing, and 2 reviews on Smashwords.

When you conduct an eBook giveaway through LibraryThing, realize every reader who requests your book may not actually read it and post a review for you online. However, it is relatively simple to post your eBook giveaway online, there is no out of pocket cost to you if you use eBook copies, and there is potential for you to get more reviews for your book. Therefore, I believe it is a worthwhile use of your time.

## #4: Storycartel.com eBook Giveaway

Story Cartel is a website that allows you to post your book on their website for readers to download and review. I have not yet used their service, but wanted to include it as an option for you. They do currently require that you pay an upfront fee of $30 in order to list your book on their site. This covers their administrative costs and also the costs of conducting a giveaway for those who request your book for review.

*Additional Resources:*

Story Cartel FAQ:
storycartel.com/faq

Register for a free account here:
storycartel.com/registration

**Tip**: Once you offer a book for review on Story Cartel, you can then send a follow-up e-mail to the list of readers who signed up to review your first book to let them know you have a new book available to review.

# CHAPTER TEN

# Develop a Book Review Program

Developing a book review program is by far our favorite method for getting reviews. We struggled for several years to get reviews until we started our book review program via an e-mail newsletter list. We highly suggest you also develop one of your own.

We have had the best response rate with the least amount of effort using this method. It will initially take time to gather your reviewers and build your list, so we encourage you to start now. You can even start building your book review program while you are writing your book.

You can see how we have set up our book review programs here:

- Books for authors:
  www.trainingauthors.com/book-reviewers

- Shelley's list for her Christian books:
  www.bodyandsoulpublishing.com/get-free-review-copies-
  of-christian-books

And here is another example from author, Laura J. Marshall:
theoldstonewall.blogspot.com/p/blog-page.html

## 6 Steps to Develop Your Own Book Review Program

**Step #1:**

Choose an e-mail list provider and set up a new list that will be used only for your book review program.

*If you do not already have an e-mail list provider, here are a few recommendations:*

**TinyLetter.com** - free but you are limited to only 2000 contacts. This is a service provided by MailChimp and is very simple to use.

**MailChimp.com** - free for up to 2000 subscribers and up to 12,000 emails per month. However prices do get expensive as your subscriber lists increases. You can see their current prices on their website at: mailchimp.com/pricing

One of the biggest disadvantages with MailChimp is they do not allow certain affiliate links or affiliate marketing in your e-mails. I have heard of people that got their accounts shut down due to using affiliate links. MailChimp states they do not ban affiliate links but they do stop e-mails with links that are on blacklists. You can find out more at: kb.mailchimp.com/article/does-mailchimp-ban-affiliate-links

**TrafficWave** - Unlimited subscribers and lists for just $17.95. Once my lists started to grow into the thousands, my Aweber fees got fairly expensive. I decided to switch my lists to Traffic Wave as they allow unlimited subscribers and lists and have been pleased so far.

Their support is not the greatest, but they do have a comprehensive help section online and a forum as well. You can find out more about TrafficWave on our blog at: www.trainingauthors.com/aweber-vs-trafficwave.

**Aweber** - $19/month for up to 500 subscribers, then prices increase as your subscribers increase. They are known for the best deliverability and reliability.

I have used Aweber and their support is excellent. If you want to have someone available to talk you through the technical issues of having an e-mail list, choose Aweber. You can call them at any time and talk directly with their support staff. I have done this several times and always received immediate answers to my questions.

**Step #2:**

Write the first e-mail your reviewers will receive. Then, make sure to add it as an autoresponder that will be sent out immediately after they confirm their subscription to your list.

Below is an example of our first e-mail in our list within TrafficWave. Feel free to use this e-mail as a template that you can modify and use for your own book reviewer program. However, please make sure to edit it with your own information.

====================

**Subject:**

\*\*FIRSTNAME\*\* - Which book would you like to start reading first?

**E-mail:**

\*\*FIRSTNAME\*\*,

Thank you so much for your interest in reviewing books for us. Honest reviews are necessary in order to participate in certain promotions, advertising and helps spread the word about our books. So we really appreciate you.

**How Review Copies Work**

1. Choose the first book you would like to read and review. You can find a complete list of our books for authors at: www.trainingauthors.com/books

Once you've decided which book you'd like to review, simply reply to this e-mail to let us know the book title you have chosen.

2. If you are on Goodreads, add the book to your collection and mark it as currently reading once you have received your free copy.

3. If at all possible, we ask that you post your review on Amazon within 2-4 weeks of receiving the book. We understand that emergencies come up and life gets busy, but we do ask you to do everything you can to keep your commitment. Please make sure to note at the end of your review that you received a free copy of this book in exchange for your honest review as this is a FTC guideline and part of Amazon's terms of service. You can simply state something like this: "Please note: I received a free copy of this book in exchange for my honest review."

4. Once you have finished posting your review, let us know which book you would like to read and review next and we will send it to you. Simply choose one of our books listed above, or wait for a new release. We'll be sending out notifications each time a new book is released and as long as you don't have any outstanding reviews - you can claim a free copy and be the first to read it.

Now the fun starts! Reply to this e-mail with the book title you would like to review.

Please note most review copies will be in eBook format. From time to time, we will offer print copies of our books. These will only be available to this list of reviewers.

*Thank you so much for your help! We really appreciate you!*

Shelley Hitz and Heather Hart
TrainingAuthors.com

====================

**Step #3:**

Set up a page for reviewers to sign up on your website or blog. On this page, give a brief description on how your book review program works and include the opt-in form for the book reviewer list you set up via your e-mail provider.

See our example at: www.trainingauthors.com/book-reviewers

If you are interested, you can sign up for our program to see exactly how it works.

**Step #4:**

Now that your book review program is set up, it is time to start promoting it. Here are a few ideas to help you grow your book review program:

1. Let your current followers know about your book review program via a blog post, Facebook posts, tweets, etc.

2.  Share about your book review program in Facebook groups, Google+ communities, and LinkedIn groups. However, be very careful to follow the group rules and do not spam.

3.  When a fan e-mails you about your book, you can give them a personal invitation to join your book review program.

4.  You can also approach people that you know enjoy your books and ask them if they would be willing to be a reviewer for you on an ongoing basis.

5.  Add a link to your book review program in the sidebar of your website or blog.

6.  If you have a general e-mail list for readers, include information about your book review program in one of the follow-up autoresponders you set up.

**Step #5:**

Send out review copies to individual reviewers as requests start to come in from your list.

We handle our review copies in two different ways.

1.  For our author books, we list the books available to review and send out review copies for any of those books to those who request them.

2. For Shelley's Christian books, she sends out review copies for new books only. This cuts down significantly on the time spent sending review copies on an ongoing basis.

You will then need to send the book file they requested via e-mail. We have created templates for the e-mails we send reviewers to save time. This is covered in depth in Part Three in the chapter, "Soliciting Reviews."

**Step #6:**

Make sure to track your review request and send follow-up e-mails to those who have not posted their review within the time you requested. We always see additional reviews posted when we send out a follow-up e-mail reminder.

In part three, Heather will share in detail how to contact reviewers including the types of review files to send, the e-mails to send, how to track your review requests, and when to follow-up with your reviewers.

# PART THREE

# Contacting Reviewers

# CHAPTER ELEVEN

# Types of Review Files to Send

Another one of the questions we receive from authors regarding reviews is, "How do I send review copies?" or "What type of review copy do I send?"

I (Heather) am part of multiple review programs for traditional publishers, and, most of the time, they let the reviewer select whether they would prefer a physical review copy or a digital eBook. Obviously digital copies are cheaper and even traditional programs seem to be leaning towards cutting out physical review copies.

For authors who are soliciting their own reviews, sending digital copies is the most economical option. Just know that there are still readers out there who won't review digital copies. It is also important that you send digital copies in a professional format. In this section, I will outline some of the different ways that you can send review copies. But first, I want to cover the topic of ARCs.

## Advance Review Copies (ARCs)

Advance review copies (or ARCs) are review copies that are made available before the book becomes available for sale, and sometimes even before it is 100% finished. These are usually labeled clearly so that the reviewers know the contents is still subject to change. They can also be referred to as a pre-release galley when in print format.

I based my own ARC notification text off of one of the galleys I received from a traditional publisher[iii]. Here is what I currently use:

**NOTE:**

This is an advance review copy.
All content herein is copyrighted (year) by Heather Hart
and is still subject to edits and changes.

You can use a version of that text or write out one of your own, but if your book is still being edited, it is always good to let your readers know. This also helps them to know that any typos they run across while reading will most likely be fixed and encourages them to review the book for its content instead of any editing errors they may find.

The galley I based mine off of also included the expected publication date of the finalized version underneath the disclaimer; i.e.:

*Book Title* will be published by publisher name
in month, year.

Once the book is available for purchase, or completely finalized, you can send out regular copies to reviewers and do not need to worry about including an ARC disclaimer.

## Digital Review Copies

As I mentioned at the beginning of this chapter, there are multiple ways to send review copies. In this section, I will focus on different ways to send digital review copies.

### 100% off Coupons

There are several companies that allow you to create coupon codes to make your eBook free or 100% off. The one we use most frequently is Smashwords. The great thing about Smashwords coupons is that they allow the reviewer to choose the type of file they want to download. They can choose between 8 different file types including a .mobi, .epub, and PDF, or they can read your book online.

### Kindle Review Copies

Sending Kindle review copies is not as easy as sending 100% off coupons from Smashwords, but you do have several options available. As we have already discussed, Amazon's terms of service state you cannot give anything in exchange for a review other than a free copy of your book. So you cannot send someone the money to buy your book. You can, however, gift them a copy directly from Amazon. When we do this, we usually lower the price to 99 cents to save us money and always start with a limited number (e.g., 10).

A cheaper way to give your readers a free Kindle review copy would be to send them a .mobi file of your book they can e-mail to their Kindle reading device. You can format .mobi files with Calibre Software (which is free), Scrivener or with the Kinstant Formatter.

If you need more information on formatting eBook, I recommend checking out this article on our website:

TrainingAuthors.com/eBooks

Another option would be to download the .mobi preview file from KDP dashboard. When you upload your book file to Kindle, they automatically convert it to .mobi for you and allow you to download that file to preview on your Kindle device. We contacted Amazon to verify that we were allowed to use their file to send to reviewers and they said yes. Here's their exact response:

====================

"You are welcome to use the .mobi file downloaded from your KDP Bookshelf to send to book reviewers.

You'll be able to download the .mobi file by doing the following:

1. Log in: kdp.amazon.com
2. Find the book you want to update, and in the "Other Book Actions" column, click "Edit book details."

3. Scroll down to the Section 6. Preview Your Book box.

4. In the 'Downloadable Previewer' select the 'Download Book Preview File' link.

You will be asked to select a location on your computer to save the file.

I hope you find this information helpful.

Thanks for using Amazon KDP."

=====================

So they are 100% okay with authors sharing that file with reviewers. Just note that if your book is enrolled in the KDP Select program, you can only send your book file to professional reviewers. We have also heard that if you enable digital rights management the .mobi file your download from KDP may not work correctly for reviewers. We personally do not use DRM, so we cannot say for certain whether or not this is true. You can read Shelley's post on the pros and cons of DRM at: thefutureofink.com/pros-and-cons-of-drm.

Once you have a file to send them, you have three options for getting that file to their Kindle device.

1. Send them the file via e-mail and they can transfer it to their Kindle via a USB cord
2. Send it via e-mail and then they can e-mail it to their Kindle.
3. You (the author) can send the .mobi file directly to their Kindle device—which is what Shelley recommends.

Sending the file to their Kindle device will save reviewers steps in the long run, but it does take a bit more setup to get started. Here's how:

Have your book reviewer add your e-mail to their list of approved e-mails in their Kindle account as follows.

1. Login to Amazon and go to "Manage Your Kindle" – www.amazon.com/myk
2. Click on the link for "Personal Document Settings"
3. Add the e-mail address of the person sending the review copy to the approved list.

Next, have your book reviewer send you their Kindle e-mail address. (Found under "Manage Your Devices" and selecting the preferred device – or you can also find the Kindle e-mail addresses under "Personal Document Settings.")

Now, all you need to do is send an e-mail to the Send-to-Kindle e-mail address with the .mobi file attached. It should automatically be sent to the Kindle device associated with that e-mail address. It is not required that you add anything in the subject line or e-mail body.

Shelley wrote a post on our website that includes all of the information on sending review copies to Kindle devices in a step-by-step format with screenshots at: www.trainingauthors.com/send-kindle-mobi-review-copy. If you want to send your reviewers more detailed instructions, you can send them to that post. Or, you can find more information about the Send-to-Kindle e-mail feature on Amazon's website at: www.amazon.com/gp/sendtokindle/email

## .epub Files

Similarly to .mobi files, .epub files can be crated to send to your re-viewers with formatting software such as the Kinstant Formatter, Calibre, or Scrivener.

If you want to use the Scrivener software, Kristen Eckstein has some Scrivener templates available. You can find them at: www.trainingauthors.com/scrivner

## PDF Review Copies

Originally, we sent PDF review copies to reviewers as default. This is a great free option, and you can customize your files to add in headers and footers so each page contains a link to your website and copyright information.

Creating PDF review copies is a pretty easy process. You simply for-mat your book file into a full page size, add in any headers and footers you want, and then if you are in a word processor (such as Microsoft Word) you should be able to click "Save As" and choose the PDF file type option. If you're using a software option that doesn't have a save as PDF option, we recommend the PDF995 software that you can download for free on their website, www.pdf995.com.

# Physical Review Copies

Sending physical review copies is more expensive than sending eBook copies. Even gifting Kindle copies to your following is easier on your marketing budget than sending a paperback to your reviewers. However, not many authors offer physical review copies, so this can make them more valuable and result in a higher request rate from potential reviewers. I personally used to only review physical books, so I know firsthand that by offering free paperbacks, you may pick up reviewers that would not have considered your book otherwise.

Another upside to sending out physical review copies is that the recipients are more likely to follow through and post a review. They will have a tangible reminder staring at them every day reminding them to get a review posted. It also gets a copy of your book into their home. So, when they are looking for new authors to read, they will have your face staring back at them. This makes it more likely for them to remember your name as an author.

How you send physical review copies will differ depending on your publishing method. If you are traditionally published, most publishing companies will send you a certain number of books that you can use for whatever you would like. You can use those as review copies, or your publisher may have your book enrolled in a review program already. So you might want to check with them first.

If you indie published your print book via CreateSpace, you can order copies through the CreateSpace dashboard one at a time and have them shipped directly to your reviewers at your cost. You won't receive any royalties on these books, but they are less expensive and CreateSpace will take care of the shipping and handling side of things for you (you do pay the shipping charges, however).

If you have used a different publishing method, you may have a box of books on hand that you can use for review copies, or you may need to check with your publisher or printer on how you can order copies for your reviewers.

If you send a physical copy of your book, we recommend including a physical letter reminding them of the review details and thanking them for helping you out. This is standard from professional review programs. I have also received notes directly from the author thanking me and sometimes a bookmark with the book cover on it. Just a little something extra to show they appreciate me as a reviewer.

*Caution:* When sending a little something extra, never send marketing material without permission. Do not assume that because they agreed to review your book, they will also hand out bookmarks or send postcards to their friends and family. One bookmark is a bonus gift, 10 is a tacky marketing tactic unless they requested or agreed to it beforehand.

## AudioBooks

If you published your audiobook through ACX, they normally give you a number of coupon codes that you can use for book marketing or collecting reviews. They include detailed instructions on how readers can claim them in the e-mail with the codes, but I will list the 5 step process here as well:

1.  Go to www.audible.com/at/redeem
2.  Enter a coupon code into the field and click "Redeem".

3. Sign in or create your audible account (free)—you can link this automatically with your Amazon account to keep from having one more account to remember.

4. Follow the instructions on the screen to have 1 credit applied to your account.

5. Click the link to the book you want (we recommending including a link to your book in the instructions you send your reviewers) and add it to your cart. When you check out you'll see an option to apply the free credit.

If you have published through ACX with an exclusive contract this is your only option for audiobook review copies, unless you want to purchase an audiobook gift copy from Amazon.

If you have recorded your own audiobook, or retained all the rights to distribute it, you can send out the finalized MP3 files for your book. You can use a software like Amazon S3 to host them online, or choose a different delivery method, but they will probably be too large to attach via e-mail. I have seen authors embed the files on their website, so readers can listen online, or click a link to download the mp3 to their computer. If you go that option, we recommend using a password protected page and possibly a flow shield for your download links.

You can learn more about publishing and marketing AudioBooks here: www.trainingauthors.com/audiobooks

# CHAPTER TWELVE

# Soliciting Reviews

We have covered quite a bit of information about getting honest reviews already in this book, but we have saved the most important part for last. In this chapter, I (Heather) am going to cover how to contact reviewers. This is where you either make or break your success when it comes to getting reviewers to actually review your book.

Shelley and I have both gotten e-mails from authors that say something like, "Hey! You're awesome. I've attached a complimentary copy of my book for you and I'd love for you to leave a review!" I like to call that an "Epic Fail." I have never reviewed one of those books. I usually just delete the e-mail without even checking to see what the title of the book was. And sending an e-mail that says, "I'd like to send you a free review copy of my book, 'Title Here.' Can you please provide me with your mailing address?" Is not much better.

When it comes to soliciting reviews the best rule of thumb is **ask first**. Do not assume someone wants to review your book. Since you want them to do something for you, it is only polite to ask them if they are willing and interested.

Your first contact with prospective reviewers should be to ask if they would be interested in reviewing your book for you. Be sure to include the book's title and a short description. After all, they won't know if it is a book they will like if they do not know what it is about.

Here is a sample e-mail that we have sent out to our book review list when soliciting reviews:

====================

**Subject:**

New Review Opportunity: Book Marketing Success Bundle

**E-mail:**

\*\*FIRSTNAME\*\*,

Shelley and I have just released our newest book for authors - but it's not all new. We've taken 5 of our eBooks and combined them into one giant bundle dedicated to helping authors succeed.

It's called the Book Marketing Success Bundle and includes the following 5 books:
Book Marketing for Beginners
Marketing Your Book on Amazon
How to Publish and Market Audiobooks

7 Book Marketing Case Studies and Other Lessons Learned
Author Publicity Pack

Now, we're reaching out to you to see if you'd be willing to review it before our launch later this month. If so, please reply to this e-mail and we'll get you a copy (review copies will be available in PDF and .mobi files).

Still not sure? You can learn more about this book on Amazon at: smarturl.it/successbundle

If you'd like a free review copy, just let us know - and no matter what you decide, we appreciate you!

Here's to your success,
Heather Hart

*Note: In order to receive a free review copy of this book, you must first have posted reviews for any other books that you have requested from us.*

=====================

If our reviewers are interested in our book we respond with another e-mail (I will talk more about that in a moment). That is just one example of an e-mail you can send.

## Other Ways to Contact Reviewers

E-mail is not your only option for soliciting reviews. We have covered in previous chapters that you can contact bloggers, post on social media, etc. to find reviewers for your book.

A social media post might look like this:

I'm looking for reviewers for my latest book, "Book Title." It's the story of... (use a short description). If you're interested in receiving a free review copy, please let me know!

For the "let me know" section, you will want to include the way you want them to contact you. If you have a review program, you might send them to the opt-in page and say, "You can sign up to get a free copy here: link" If you just want them to e-mail you, you can leave your e-mail address, or let them send you a message via the social media platform (just make sure that you can send and receive messages first).

Here is an example that I posted in a Facebook authors group for one of our books:

We're looking for reviews on our latest book for authors, "Book Marketing Success Bundle: 5 Books for Authors." Would any of you be willing to review it for us? It's a combination of 5 of our previous books, so you may have even already read some or all of it. Here's the link to check it out:

www.amazon.com/dp/B00HND2HWG

If you want a review copy - just let me know!

If they requested a copy, I sent them a message on Facebook with everything they needed to know.

If you are contacting a blog reviewer, you will want to introduce yourself first. Then let them know how you found their blog, or how long you have been following them before you jump into your request. You might comment on a recent post or complement the concept of their blog. Just make sure you are genuine. Phony compliments never win fans. Be specific, not generic and don't send the same e-mail introduction to each and every blog owner. Since you are asking them to spend several hours doing you a favor, you can take 5-10 minutes to personalize the request.

After you have let them know who you are and that you know who they are, you can then let them know you are looking for reviews for your book (include the title and a short description). Let them know why you are asking them—is it a good fit for their audience? Did they recently blog about the same topic? Have you worked together before?

Then let them know the terms you are offering. What file types you have available and the time frame you are looking at. If this blog frequently reviews books, you will want to check to see if they have a contact form specifically for review requests and if they have any of their own terms posted.

Many reviewers will state their turnaround time, preferred genres, etc. on their site. So check for that before contacting them. If you do not take the time to read through what they want, there is a good chance your request will get deleted.

## Sending Review Copies

Once you are ready to send review copies to those who have requested them, there are a few things you want to make sure you include in your message.

First, the Federal Trade Commission (FTC) requires reviewers to add a note to their review that they received a free copy in exchange for an honest review. The FTC's most recent reports[iv] say that both the company and the reviewer can be fined if this is not disclosed, so it is very important to ask your reviewers to add a disclaimer.

Here is one example that we have used:

> Please make sure to note at the end of your review that you received a free copy of this book in exchange for your honest review as this is an FTC guideline and part of Amazon's terms of service. You can simply state something like this: "I was provided a free copy of this book by the author in exchange for my honest review."

Some of the companies that I review for ask you to go into more detail and state that while you received a free copy in exchange for a review, all the opinions and ideas expressed in your review are your own. But the FTC doesn't specify wording, they just want to make sure that the relationship between the product owner and the reviewer is disclosed; i.e., they got a free copy in exchange for leaving a review.

The next thing you will want to include in your e-mail to the reviewer are the links to where you want the reviews posted. We recommend including two links. Amazon and Goodreads are the two that we generally focus on first. So we include the direct link to our book on those sites.

You want to make reviewing your book as easy as possible for your reviewers. If you have created separate digital files for reviewers, you might even include these links directly at the end of the book so, when they finish reading, they can click straight over to leave their reviews. You will still want to note within the e-mail where you want the reviews posted and include the links there as well, but you can also mention that the links are included in the back of the book for their convenience.

We do not recommend that you ask them to post their review in more than 3 places, or include more than 3 links. You do not want to overwhelm your reviewers. Sometimes an author's enthusiasm can quickly take advantage of a reader's willingness to review their book—we don't mean to, it just happens—but just because your book is available on Amazon, Kobo, Barnes & Noble, Smashwords, the iBook store, and Sony, doesn't mean that you should include links to all of them. Pick 2 or 3.

Lastly, you will want to reiterate your time frame and attach your files if needed (it is always embarrassing to have to send a second e-mail with the files attached, so be sure double check this). If you are sending a gift copy from Amazon, you will want to send a separate e-mail letting them know that you've sent it and include all of the information.

Here's an example of an e-mail we have sent out to our reviewers:

====================

**FIRSTNAME**,

Thank you for requesting a review copy of our book, Author Publicity Pack: Resources to Help You Take Your Book Marketing to the Next Level.

I've attached a PDF copy for you to review. If you prefer, you can download other versions from Smashwords using the coupon below:

Coupon Code: AP39H
Expires: March 15, 2013

www.Smashwords.com/books/view/287168

If at all possible we ask that you post your review on Amazon prior to our official launch on 3/5/13. We also ask that if you are on Goodreads that you would mark it as "currently-reading" and then post your review there as well once you've finished reading it. We really appreciate your help!

Please make sure to note at the end of your review that you received a free copy of this book in exchange for your honest review as this is a FTC guideline and part of Amazon's terms of service. You can simply state something like this: "I was provided this book by Body and Soul Publishing in exchange for my review."

Here are the links to post your review online:

Amazon: www.amazon.com/dp/B00BGXAADC

Goodreads: www.Goodreads.com/book/show/17381296-author-publicity-pack

Thank you so much for your help! We hope you find some new resources to put to use from this book.

====================

If you asked your following what type of file they would like to receive. You might use something like this example:

====================

**FIRSTNAME**,

Thank you so much for requesting to review my newest eBook. I really appreciate you!

I've attached a .mobi review copy for you as requested.

Once you've read the book, I'd appreciate it if you could post your review at the following places:

Amazon: www.amazon.com/dp/B00GP048KC

Goodreads: www.Goodreads.com/book/show/18815127-holiday-marketing

If at all possible, please submit your review within 2-4 weeks (or as soon as possible). And as always, make sure to note at the end of your review that you received a free copy of this book in exchange for your honest review as this is a FTC guideline and part of Amazon's terms of service. You can simply state something like this: "I was provided this book by the author in exchange for my review."

Thanks for your help!

=====================

*Note:* When working with a new reviewer, we will often include the link to Amazon's Send to Kindle instructions that we mentioned earlier.

The wording you use in your e-mail is entirely up to you, we just wanted to show you an example of what an e-mail could look like when it includes all the information needed.

After you have sent out your review copies we recommend waiting until close to the end of the time frame you gave your reviewers and then sending a reminder to those who have not yet posted a review.

This is where tracking your reviews comes in as important. If someone has fulfilled their commitment and posted their review, sending them reminders is a bad idea. So let's go ahead and move on to the next chapter where I will cover different strategies for tracking reviews, then I will cover sending follow-up messages.

# CHAPTER THIRTEEN

# Tracking Reviews

When soliciting reviews, tracking which reviewers followed through and which reviewers did not is important for multiple reasons. First, we recommend sending a follow-up message to reviewers who have not posted their reviews in the time frame you requested. If you are not tracking your reviews, you won't know who has posted a review and who has not. And if you plan on publishing multiple books, you want to know who to contact in the future and who to pass on when sending new review copies. Our policy is that reviewers cannot request a new book to review until they have posted the review for the previous book they requested. If you do not have a way to track your reviews, you won't know who is eligible and who is not.

Originally, I tracked reviews by keeping e-mails in my inbox. I would keep the request e-mail from them until they posted their review and then delete it. Obviously this is not the best way to go about it.

Shelley and I currently use an Excel spreadsheet. We have 6 columns: reviewer name, e-mail address, title of book they are reviewing, the date we sent the book, whether or not we have sent a reminder, and their amazon handle.

When we send a reviewer a new book, we make sure their line has a white background. Once they post their review, we highlight their line in green to clear them for another book. If they fail to post a review, even after being reminded, we highlight their line in red so we know not to send them any more free books unless we see a review for that book come through.

This works really well for us. Whenever someone sends us an e-mail that they have posted their review, we update our spreadsheet. We also check our reviews on Amazon periodically through our Amazon author central accounts to check for new reviews (more on this in just a moment). We share our Excel template in our Book Marketing Survival Guide Tool Kit. You can learn more about how to gain access it on our website at: www.trainingauthors.com/toolkit

If you only have one or two books, you might consider keeping a running text document that has a list of people you have sent review copies to and then check them off as the reviews are posted. We managed our reviews this way at first and simply kept a separate document for each book. It is an easy way to track reviews on a book-by-book basis.

Another option for tracking your reviews is to use the system created by Kristen Eckstein. Her system helps you track all the reviews for all of your book titles in one place and is available for just $7. You can learn more about it at: www.trainingauthors.com/reviewtracker

## Checking Reviews via Author Central

Checking for new reviews via your Amazon author central account is really easy. If you do not already have an author central account, we highly recommend setting one up. You can learn more about it at: authorcentral.amazon.com

Once you are logged into your account, you can easily check for new reviews on all of your books by clicking on the "Customer Reviews" tab at the top of your screen. It will automatically pull up all of the reviews on your books from newest to oldest. It even marks ones you have not seen before with the word *"New!"* in bright red letters. A quick skim through that can tell you who has left a review and who has not. If you only want to see reviews on a certain book, you can pull it up on Amazon.

Amazon reviews are currently the only reviews we track. However, if you are pushing for reviews on other platforms, you will want to check those platforms for reviews as well or instead. Most reviews can be pulled up by going to the sales page for your book. You will want to make sure they are displayed in order of date posted (versus most helpful), so you can check for new additions.

What do you do when someone does not post a review? We are going to cover following up with reviewers in the next chapter.

# CHAPTER FOURTEEN

# Following Up
# with Reviewers

We have found that sending a follow-up message to reviewers who have not posted a review can double the response rate. Reviewers will sometimes forget, or lose the links, to post the review. They are busy just like us. Sending a simple reminder can make a huge difference.

However, when sending a reminder, it is important to remember not to harass your reviewers. One reminder should be enough. We recommend waiting either 2 weeks, or until a few days before the deadline you gave them (e.g., if you wanted it posted before your launch on the 29th, we would recommend e-mailing them between the 20th and 25th).

A typical follow-up e-mail might look as follows:

====================

**Subject:**

{Reminder} - Just checking in on your review of "Book Marketing for Beginners"

**E-mail:**

Hey **FIRSTNAME**,

I'm doing a book launch next week for my book, "Book Marketing for Beginners." You had requested a review copy and I was wondering if you've had time to read through it yet?

If at all possible, I would really appreciate it if you could post your review before the 25th as that is the day of my launch. It is a short eBook (50 pages) and yet packed full of ideas for your marketing promotions.

Here are the links to post your review if you need them again:

Amazon: www.amazon.com/dp/B00FARPGZW

Goodreads: hwww.Goodreads.com/book/show/18519955-book-marketing-for-beginners

Thank you so much for your help! I hope you learn from the tips I share in this book.

====================

As you can see we like to keep it short and sweet. A reminder that they agreed to review the book, the deadline, and the links to post their review.

Sometimes you will get responses saying they have already posted a review. If you get one of those, be sure to send a response thanking them for reading your book and for their review. I always like to read what they wrote in their review before sending a thank you, so I can personalize it. I might say, "I'm so glad you found it helpful!" or reference something else they mentioned in their review to show them that I really do appreciate them.

And as I said, make sure not to harass your reviewers. We do not recommend sending more than one follow-up message, even if they still do not post a review. Reviews are not worth bad publicity, and harassing readers is never a good idea.

If they request another review copy in the future, you can let them know you have looked, but cannot find the review they wrote for the last book you sent to them. I recommend politely asking for a link to their previous review, and letting them know as soon as you get it, you will gladly send them a copy of your most recent book.

# Conclusion

We have covered a TON of information within the pages of this book to help you get more honest reviews. When you apply this advice to your own books, we believe it will yield results.

Therefore, we encourage you to take action on what you learned. Choose at least one way to get more reviews from this book and then do it. We are cheering you on!

*To your success,*

Shelley Hitz and Heather Hart
TrainingAuthors.com

P.S. As you know, reviews are gold to authors. If you have found this book helpful, would you consider leaving an honest review on Amazon.com?

# ABOUT THE AUTHORS

Shelley Hitz and Heather Hart work as a team to help authors succeed. They have been working together since 2009 and have been referred to as the "writer's dynamic duo". One of the ways they help authors is by sharing their about their own experiences in the book industry.

## Shelley Hitz

Shelley Hitz is an award-winning and internationally best-selling author. She is the owner of TrainingAuthors.com and is passionate about helping authors succeed in publishing and marketing their books.

And she teaches from personal experience. Shelley has been writing and publishing books since 2008 and has published over 30 books including print, eBook and audio book formats.

## Heather Hart

Heather Hart is a book marketing expert, internationally best-selling author, and is the manager of TrainingAuthors.com. With the heart of an author, Heather enjoys working from home where she spends her days typing away at her computer, brainstorming new marketing ideas, and encouraging those around her.

Her desire is to help others successfully publish and market their books while continuing to author, contribute to, and market multiple book marketing and faith-based books herself – and have fun doing it.

Access Their FREE Author Training Here:
www.TrainingAuthors.com/Newsletter

See A Complete List Of Their Books For Authors Here:
www.TrainingAuthors.com/Books

## Connect with Shelley and Heather Online

www.facebook.com/trainingauthors

www.twitter.com/trainingauthors

www.youtube.com/trainingauthors

# ADDITIONAL RESOURCES

## Book Marketing Survival Guide Tool Kit

Access our database of templates, trainings and more with our Survival Guide Tool Kit. Find out more here:
www.trainingauthors.com/toolkit

## Our Books for Authors

We have an entire library of books for authors, including books on publishing and marketing. Check out the entire list here:
www.trainingauthors.com/books

## Recommended Outsourcers for Authors

If you need help with the technical side of publishing and marketing your books, consider outsourcing to one of our recommended providers here:
www.trainingauthors.com/recommended-outsourcers-for-authors

## Tools and Resources We Use and Recommend

Check out the tools we use and recommend for writing, publishing and marketing here:
www.trainingauthors.com/resources

# NOTES

[i] Gesenhues, Amy. "Survey: 90% Of Customers Say Buying Decisions Are Influenced By Online Reviews." Posted Apr 9, 2013. *Marketing Land. marketingland.com.* (Accessed April 2014.)

[ii] Kellogg, Carolyn. "Why is Amazon deleting writers' reviews of other authors' books?" November 2, 2012. *Los Angeles Times | Books. www.latimes.com/features/books/jacketcopy.* (Accessed April 2014.)

[iii] Ralya, Sandy. *The Beautiful Wife: Focused on Christ, Fulfilled in Marriage.* Pre-Release Galley. Kregel Publications. Actual book published February 2012.

[iv] Federal Trade Commission. 16 CFR Part 255. "Guides Concerning the Use of Endorsements and Testimonials in Advertising." www.ftc.gov/sites/default/files/attachments/press-releases/ftc-publishes-final-guides-governing-endorsements-testimonials/091005revisedendorsementguides.pdf. (Accessed April 2014)

Made in the USA
Charleston, SC
20 January 2017